Stormy W...

Contents

2		Clouds
4		Rain
6		Wind
8		Thunder and Lightning
10		After the Storm

Clouds

Last week we had a storm. On Tuesday morning clouds rolled in. They moved quickly across the sky.

In the afternoon the clouds grew darker. Dark grey clouds blocked out the sun.

Rain

Then it began to rain.
The rain poured down.
Everyone needed umbrellas.

The road near my house was covered in water. The cars had to drive slowly.

Wind

On Wednesday I looked out the window. It was still raining. It was also windy.

The wind was very strong. It looked like our tree was going to blow over. It was amazing.

Thunder and Lightning

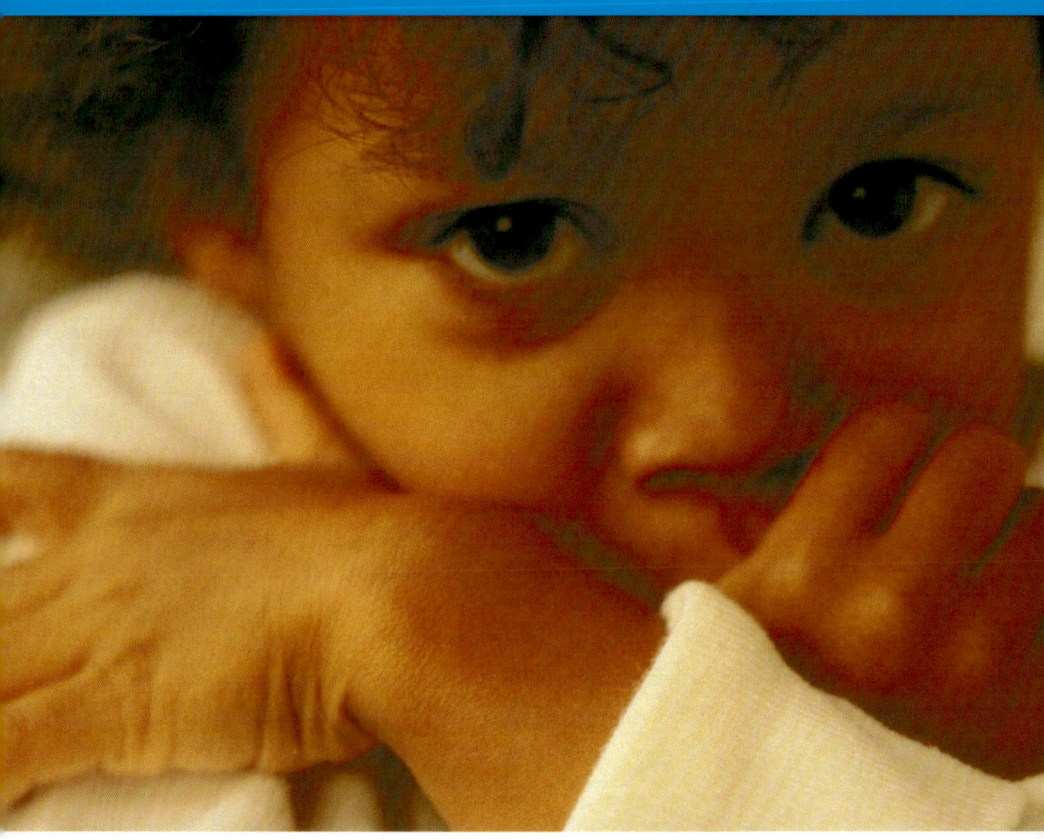

That night there was a thunderstorm. The thunder cracked and rumbled. My sister was scared.

The lightning flashed. It lit up the sky. The dog howled. It was scared too!

After the Storm

On Thursday it stopped raining. The storm did a lot of damage. A tree fell onto the road.

The river also flooded over the road.
I couldn't get to school!

Storm timeline

Tuesday
- morning
- afternoon
- evening

Wednesday
- morning
- night